Yes, Dear,
There Really Is a
Devil

CREATED BY:
Chris Rader & Johnnie Coley

CONCEPT SKETCH DESIGN:
Erin McKay

ILLUSTRATIONS BY:
Sonny Heston

PO BOX 3687
CLEBURNE, TX 76033
HOPKINSPUBLISHING.COM

COPYRIGHT © 2015
ISBN-10: 1-62080-062-4
ISBN-13: 978-1-62080-062-1
LIBRARY OF CONGRESS CONTROL NUMBER: 2015958691
VERSION 2.0

EBOOK:
ISBN-10: 1-62080-063-2
ISBN-13: 978-1-62080-063-8

ALL RIGHTS RESERVED. THIS BOOK OR PARTS THEREOF MAY NOT BE REPRODUCED IN ANY FORM WITHOUT WRITTEN PERMISSION FROM THE PUBLISHER.

"SCRIPTURE QUOTATIONS ARE FROM THE HOLY BIBLE, ENGLISH STANDARD VERSION® (ESV®), COPYRIGHT © 2001 BY CROSSWAY, A PUBLISHING MINISTRY OF GOOD NEWS PUBLISHERS. USED BY PERMISSION. ALL RIGHTS RESERVED."

DISCOVER OTHER TITLES
BY HOPKINS PUBLISHING
HOPKINSPUBLISHING.COM

DEDICATION

The idea for this book came while trying to explain the reality of the devil to my four-year-old son. After searching for a book and not finding what I was looking for, I decided to write one myself. After putting my thoughts on paper and drawing stick figures, I was blessed to meet a talented artist named Erin McKay and Johnnie Coley, a devoted Christian author who helped me move forward with my ideas.

My greatest dedication is to God, who's word, the Bible, gave me the inspiration for this project. It is also dedicated to all the parents, grandparents, and caregivers who desire to teach their children the truth of God's word. Children are never too young to start learning about God. In Psalm 127:3, the psalmist says: "Children are a heritage from the Lord." God has entrusted us with our children - such precious gifts - to raise them up as warriors unto Him. I believe we must value the minds and souls of these precious gifts that we have been given, by sharing God's truth with them in regard to the battles they will face in this life.

I hope this book is a blessing for you, the reader, and all children. To God be the glory!

Chris Rader

FOREWARD

What courage it must have taken to initiate the subject of dealing with the devil in a children's book. This type of book is fairly non-existent. One of the realities is that children must also ready themselves for the battles they will face with Satan. Chris' godly values and respect for the truth have given her a tenacious stand in this matter and, for that, I am very proud of her.

Chris, may your golden ride through this experience be like the horse in the open country (Isaiah 63:13). Sour as if no one exists in the sky except for you. May young lives be changed because God's word and your book alerted them to the enemy early in their development.

Remember: "While the horse is ready for battle, the victory rests with the Lord always" (Proverbs 21:31). It has been amazing to watch the unfolding of this project in your life and to see it in full operation as you teach your children. Your children are blessed because your heart is open to God's truth about the devil. Continue to teach and uncover the devil's tactics and share them with the little hearts God has placed in your path. May there always be a bench for us to sit on and talk about God's wonderful truth.

Johnnie Coley, MS
AUTHOR, PARENTING WITH POWER

THERE'S SO MUCH TO DO, MANY CHOICES TO MAKE.
BETTER MAKE IT GOOD, BECAUSE YOUR SOUL IS AT STAKE.

SUBMIT YOURSELVES THEREFORE TO GOD. RESIST THE DEVIL, AND HE WILL FLEE FROM YOU. DRAW NEAR TO GOD, AND HE WILL DRAW NEAR TO YOU.

James 4:7-8a

THE DEVIL WANTS YOU TO MAKE A BAD CHOICE. SO LISTEN TO GOD AND OBEY HIS WISE VOICE.

BUT EACH PERSON IS TEMPTED WHEN HE IS LURED AND ENTICED BY HIS OWN DESIRE.

James 1:14

GOD CREATED US HUMAN, OUR BLOOD IS THE SAME.
GOD LOVES US SO MUCH, THAT'S WHY JESUS CAME.

SO GOD CREATED MAN IN HIS OWN IMAGE,
IN THE IMAGE OF GOD HE CREATED HIM;
MALE AND FEMALE HE CREATED THEM.

Genesis 1:27

THE DEVIL IS MEAN, HE WANTS YOU TO FALL. JESUS IS WITH US, HE'LL HELP YOU STAND TALL.

THE THIEF COMES ONLY TO STEAL AND KILL AND DESTROY. I (JESUS) CAME THAT THEY MAY HAVE LIFE AND HAVE IT ABUNDANTLY.

John 10:10

THE RIGHT PATH IS NARROW, NO BACKPACK WILL FIT.
IT MAY NOT BE EASY, BUT PLEASE DO NOT QUIT!

FOR THE GATE IS NARROW AND THE WAY IS HARD THAT
LEADS TO LIFE, AND THOSE WHO FIND IT ARE FEW.

Matthew 7:14

THE DEVIL IS AIMING, BE QUICK AND BE READY! YOUR SHIELD OF FAITH WILL KEEP YOU STEADY.

IN ALL CIRCUMSTANCES TAKE UP THE SHIELD OF FAITH, WITH WHICH YOU CAN EXTINGUISH ALL THE FLAMING DARTS OF THE EVIL ONE;

Ephesians 6:16

NOW X-RAY YOUR HEART AND ALWAYS BE REAL.
WE MAY FOOL OTHERS, BUT GOD KNOWS THE DEAL.

"FOR OUT OF THE ABUNDANCE OF THE HEART THE MOUTH SPEAKS. THE GOOD PERSON OUT OF HIS GOOD TREASURE BRINGS FORTH GOOD, AND THE EVIL PERSON OUT OF HIS EVIL TREASURE BRINGS FORTH EVIL.

Matthew 12:34b-35

PUT ON YOUR ARMOR, AND GET IN GOD'S ZONE! THE DEVIL WILL GRUMBLE AND LEAVE YOU ALONE!

"FINALLY, BE STRONG IN THE LORD AND IN THE STRENGTH OF HIS MIGHT. PUT ON THE WHOLE ARMOR OF GOD, THAT YOU MAY BE ABLE TO STAND AGAINST THE SCHEMES OF THE DEVIL."

Ephesians 6:10-11

A NOTE TO CAREGIVERS

BELOW ARE SOME EXTRA IDEAS AND RESOURCES TO HELP YOU FURTHER TEACH HOW TO AVOID THE WILES OF THE DEVIL. THESE MIGHT BE USEFUL IN A FAMILY DEVOTIONAL OR IN A BIBLE CLASS SETTING.

READ 2 TIMOTHY 2:15 AND DISCUSS THE IMPORTANCE OF REGULAR BIBLE STUDY. HOW DO YOU RIGHTLY HANDLE THE WORD OF TRUTH?

READ EPHESIANS 6:13-17 WITH YOUR CHILDREN. TALK ABOUT WHEN A SOLDIER WEARS ARMOR IT IS TO PROTECT HIM AND THAT WE NEED TO WEAR SPIRITUAL ARMOR TO PROTECT OURSELVES FROM SIN.

PRINT OUT THE FREE ARMOR OF GOD COLORING SHEET AND HELP YOUR CHILDREN LABEL THE PIECES OF ARMOR AS READ IN EPHESIANS 6.

THE ARMOR OF GOD

IT IS A GOOD IDEA TO UNDERLINE THE WORDS TRUTH, RIGHTEOUSNESS, GOSPEL OF PEACE, FAITH, SALVATION, AND WORD OF GOD IN YOUR BIBLE. THESE ARE WORDS THAT CAN BE STUDIED FURTHER AS YOUR CHILD GETS OLDER.

READ PSALM 119:11 AND TALK ABOUT WHAT IT MEANS TO STORE UP GOD'S WORD IN YOUR HEART.

READ HEBREWS 4:12 AND TALK ABOUT HOW GOD'S WORD IS LIKE A SWORD.

A WORD FROM THE AUTHORS

THANK YOU FOR PURCHASING *YES, DEAR, THERE REALLY IS A DEVIL*, AND PASSING THE WORD TO OTHER PARENTS WHO DESIRE TO TEACH THEIR CHILDREN THE TRUTH OF GOD'S WORD. IF YOU WOULD LIKE MORE INFORMATION ABOUT THE AUTHORS, CONTACT CHRIS RADER AT YESDEAR2013@AOL.COM OR JOHNNIE COLEY AT WWW.JOHNNIECOLEY.COM. IF THIS BOOK WAS A BLESSING TO YOU, PLEASE CONSIDER POSTING A REVIEW ON AMAZON.

Chris Rader & Johnnie Coley

Made in the USA
Coppell, TX
15 January 2025